Paraguay

Paraguay

BY BYRON AUGUSTIN

*Enchantment of the World
Second Series*

Children's Press®

A Division of Scholastic Inc.

NEW YORK   TORONTO   LONDON   AUCKLAND   SYDNEY
MEXICO CITY   NEW DELHI   HONG KONG
DANBURY, CONNECTICUT

Frontispiece: Ruins of La Santisima Trinidad de Paraná

Consultant: Alice C. Sagehorn, PhD, Sagehorn Associates

Please note: All statistics are as up-to-date as possible at the time of publication.

Book production by Herman Adler Design

Library of Congress Cataloging-in-Publication Data

Augustin, Byron.
 Paraguay / by Byron Augustin.
   p. cm. — (Enchantment of the world. Second series.)
 Includes bibliographical references and index.
 ISBN 0-516-23675-X
 1. Paraguay—Juvenile literature. I. Title. II. Series.
 F2668.5.A94 2005
 989.2—dc22   2005000751

Acknowledgments

I would like to acknowledge my wife, Rebecca, who supported this project with patience and understanding. I am grateful to Dr. Lawrence Estaville, chairman of the Texas State University Department of Geography, for his careful academic content editing of the text. Jake Kubena, my trusted graduate assistant at Texas State University, completed the tedious task of metric conversions and carefully edited the manuscript. A final note of thanks is extended to my dear friend Angelika Wahl for typing this manuscript.

This book is dedicated to the more than 25,000 students who have been enrolled in my university geography classes over the past forty years.

Contents

Cover photo:
A rug seller in
Asunción

The Cordillera
de Amambay

A Paraguayan grandmother and her grandson

The Island

PARAGUAY IS SOMETIMES CALLED "AN ISLAND SURROUNDED by land." It is located deep in the heart of the South American continent, and not one of its borders touches an ocean. Yet water in the form of rivers shapes 80 percent of Paraguay's borders. These rivers have provided a route into the region since humans first arrived there.

People have lived in Paraguay for thousands of years. The Guaraní lived in the lush forests of the eastern part of the country. They had no trouble finding food. The rivers were

Opposite: **Still waters of the Río Paraguay**

The Río Paraguay forms a portion of the border between Paraguay and Argentina.

filled with fish, and the forests abounded with wildlife. But tribes living in western Paraguay had a harder time. They struggled to survive in a land of extremes.

Guaraní religious beliefs included the idea that a fair-skinned, blue-eyed visitor would change their lives. Little did they know just how completely outsiders would change their world.

Spanish and Portuguese explorers arrived in Paraguay early in the sixteenth century. At first, they had little interest in the country because it had no gold or silver. But the Spanish had to pass through Paraguay to get to Peru, where the incredible wealth of the Inca Empire was found. Asunción, Paraguay's capital, became an important center for the Spanish rule of South America.

Most of the Spaniards who settled in Paraguay did not bring their families. Instead, they intermarried with the local Indians. The trend continued, and today Paraguay is 95 percent *mestizo*, people with a mixed Indian and Spanish background.

The Incas' kingdom was rich with gold, which they sometimes made into objects like this llama.

Culturally, Paraguay reflects this mixed ethnic heritage. Both Guaraní Indian and European traditions have influenced Paraguayan music, art, and writing. Early Spanish missionaries worked tirelessly to convert the native population to Roman Catholicism. Today, 95 percent of Paraguayans are Catholic. There is a strong current of Indian religious beliefs just below the surface, however.

Almost all Paraguayans are Catholic.

Paraguay has seen its share of trouble. Since becoming independent from Spain in 1811, it has been dominated by dictators. These dictators helped isolate Paraguay from the rest of the world, but a new constitution written in 1992 is providing a sense of hope for the future. The country has many treasures waiting to be explored. Its people are among the most generous and helpful in the world. Paraguay's citizens are ready to make their mark in Latin America and the world beyond.

Paraguay is filled with friendly faces.

East and West

ARAGUAY WAS LONG ONE OF THE MOST INACCESSIBLE NATIONS in South America. Located in the heart of the continent, the country has no direct access to the sea. Exploring Paraguay was difficult because much of the country has a harsh environment. Powerful rivers were difficult to cross. Swamps and marshes were filled with poisonous snakes and swarming insects. Endless plains of thorny brush seared by scorching temperatures and drought blocked human settlement. Nature has proved a tough opponent for the hardy people who have tried to make a life for themselves in Paraguay.

Opposite: **Lake Ypacarai**

Parts of Paraguay receive little rain, making it difficult for humans to live there.

Paraguay's Geographic Features

Highest Elevation: Near Villarrica, 2,762 feet (842 m)

Lowest Elevation: Junction of the Río Paraguay and the Río Paraná 150 feet (46 m)

Largest City: Asunción, population 539,200

Longest River: Río Paraguay either borders or passes through Paraguay for 750 miles (1,200 km)

Lowest Average Annual Temperature: 69°F (20.5°C) in Ciudad del Este

Highest Average Annual Temperature: 77°F (25°C) in Bahía Negra

Lowest Recorded Temperature: 23°F (–5°C) in Mariscal Estigarriba

Highest Recorded Temperature: 110°F (43.3°C) in Mariscal Estigarriba

Largest Swamp: Estero Patino, 600 square miles (1,500 sq km)

Largest National Park: Defensores del Chaco, 3,000 square miles (7,800 sq km)

Paraguay is one of the smaller countries in South America, with an area of 157,048 square miles (406,752 square kilometers). The nation is about the same size as California or the combined areas of Labrador and Newfoundland in Canada. Paraguay is nestled between three South American giants. Argentina is to the south and west. Bolivia is to the north. Brazil is to the east.

Paraguay is generally flat, with areas of rolling hills and broad valleys. Eighty percent of the country is less than 1,000 feet (300 meters) above sea level. The highest point, near Villarrica, is only 2,762 feet (842 m) above sea level. The lowest elevation, 150 feet (46 m), is where the Río Paraguay and Río Paraná meet along the southwest border.

Most of Paraguay is covered with low hills.

The Chaco is a vast grassland with few people and almost no roads.

Two Different Landscapes

The Río Paraguay slices through central Paraguay from the north to the south. It divides the country into two distinct regions. East of the Río Paraguay is an area called the Paranena. It makes up about 40 percent of the nation's total land area. Ninety-seven percent of Paraguayans live in the Paranena. West of the Río Paraguay is a vast inhospitable plain known as the Chaco. The Chaco region covers 60 percent of Paraguay's land area but is home to only 3 percent of the country's citizens.

The Paranena

Most of the highest elevations in Paraguay are located along its eastern border with Brazil. The region is part of the Paraná Plateau, which stretches into Brazil. Elevations in this area range from 1,000 to 2,000 feet (300 to 600 m) above sea level.

In Paraguay, the Paraná Plateau includes three small ranges of hills, or *cordilleras*, called the Cordillera de Amambay, the Cordillera de Mbaracayú, and the Cordillera de Caaguazu. Though they are not particularly tall, Paraguayans think of the cordilleras as mountain ranges because the rest of the country is so flat. The Paraná Plateau is made of volcanic rock from ancient lava flows. Its reddish-brown soil is quite fertile.

The Cordillera de Amambay rises in northeastern Paraguay, near the Brazilian border.

A gently rolling landscape stretches to the west of the Paraná Plateau. This region includes open plains, broad valleys, and flat-topped hills just 20 to 30 feet (6 to 9 m) high. Asunción, the nation's capital, lies in this region, along the banks of the Río Paraguay. The area surrounding Asunción is one of the most densely settled agricultural regions in the country.

The southwest corner of the Paranena is marshy. The Neembucu Plain is dotted with low depressions. Its soil does not drain well, so it almost always floods during the rainy season. Insects love this swampland, but humans avoid it.

The land near Asunción is quite flat.

The *palo barracho*, or bottle tree, thrives in the Chaco. Its swelled trunk stores water.

The Chaco

The Chaco is one of the last great empty spaces on Earth's surface. It stretches across northern Argentina, southeastern Bolivia, and western Paraguay. Beginning at the western bank of the Río Paraguay, the Paraguayan Chaco extends toward the Andes Mountains in Argentina. It is largely unsuitable for human settlement, but many unique species of plants and animals thrive there.

The Chaco is a flat plain formed from sediment that washed off the eastern slopes of the Andes. Most of the Chaco is less than 1,000 feet (300 m) above sea level. The grayish soil has a high salt content and generally is not good for growing crops.

In the Chaco, rivers have an irregular flow. In the dry season, the rivers run dry. In the rainy season, they overflow their banks and create large swamps and marshes. As much as 15 percent of the Chaco may be covered with water during the rainy season. The Estero Patino, Paraguay's largest swamp, is located in the southeastern corner of the Chaco near the border with Argentina.

The Chaco has not changed much in the past thousand years. The region attracts few visitors. There are no major cities and only one major paved road.

Parts of the Chaco flood during the rainy season, and hyacinths flourish.

Liquid Borders

Rivers define 80 percent of Paraguay's borders with its neighbors. The three most prominent rivers are the Río Paraná, the Río Paraguay, and the Río Pilcomayo.

The Río Paraná has its source in the highlands of Brazil. It flows for 3,030 miles (4,875 km) before it reaches the Río de la Plata near Buenos Aires, Argentina. Large ships can travel up the Río Paraná all the way to Encarnación, in southeastern Paraguay. It can be a dangerous river, however. Floodwaters sometimes rise as much as 16 feet (5 m) in twenty-four hours.

The Río Paraná is famous for the dams along its course that produce huge amounts of hydroelectric power. The Itaipú and Yacyretá are the second- and fourth-largest hydroelectric projects in the world. Itaipú was a team project between Brazil and Paraguay, while Yacyretá was a joint undertaking between Argentina and Paraguay.

The Río Paraguay begins in Brazil and flows for 1,584 miles (2,549 km) until it joins the Río Paraná near Corrientes, Argentina. Along the way, the river slices through the middle of Paraguay. Paraguayans call it the "liquid spinal cord of

A Treasure Lost

At one time, more water poured over the Guaíra Falls than over almost any waterfall in the world. Millions of gallons of water thundered through a narrow canyon that the Río Paraná (right) cut through the Mbaracayú Mountains. The water dropped 375 feet (114 m) over 18 small falls as it was squeezed through a gorge. The violently churning water created a roar that could be heard 20 miles (30 km) away.

When the Itaipú Dam was completed in 1991, a huge lake formed behind it. The Guaíra Falls were completely submerged beneath the lake's surface. One of nature's most powerful and beautiful creations was lost.

The Río Paraguay separates the Chaco from the Paranena.

the country." Asunción, the capital of Paraguay, is the major port on the river. Ships leaving Asunción can travel on the Río Paraguay and Río Paraná southward to the Atlantic Ocean. The Río Paraguay is a vital route for Paraguay's exports and imports.

Paraguay's longest international border is formed by the Río Pilcomayo. The river cuts through the Chaco, separating Argentina from Paraguay. It is a sluggish river, with thick marshes. When it floods, much of its water feeds into the Estero Patino swamp. The marshes along its banks attract large numbers of birds. In fact, *Pilcomayo* is an Indian word meaning "river of birds."

All of Paraguay lies south of the equator. Because of this, seasons there are the opposite of those in the Northern Hemisphere. Summer is in January and February, and winter is in July and August. Spring and fall do not really exist as distinct seasons. April and September serve as short transitions between the two major seasons.

The Paranena region has a humid subtropical climate, much like southern Florida. Average temperatures are in the low to mid-70s Fahrenheit (low 20s Celsius). The entire region gets a lot of rain, but the east is the wettest. It gets about 20 inches (50 centimeters) more rain than the western Paranena.

The climate in the Chaco varies greatly, from warm and humid in the southeast to semiarid in the west. Weather is much less predictable in the Chaco than in eastern Paraguay.

Eastern Paraguay gets as much as 60 inches (150 cm) of rain per year.

Stunted trees grow in mudflats in the Chaco.

In general, temperatures are 5° to 10°F (2.5° to 5.5°C) warmer than in the Paranena, and temperature changes are generally more extreme. The hottest official temperature, 110°F (43.3°C), and the coldest official temperature, 23°F (–5°C), were both recorded in the western Chaco at Mariscal Estigarriba.

Rainfall in the Chaco averages 40 inches (100 cm) in the east but just 20 inches (50 cm) in the west. Winters tend to be dry, with some periods of severe drought lasting six to eight months. Summers, on the other hand, sometimes see violent thunderstorms with lightning, high winds, and heavy rain. Some regions of the Chaco are deserts in the winters and swamps in the summers.

Floods are a major danger in Paraguay. They often destroy homes.

Nature's Violence

Paraguay does not experience volcanic eruptions, earthquakes, or landslides. Instead, most natural disasters there are caused by weather. Flooding causes more loss of life and property than any other type of natural disaster. Hail and high winds wreak havoc on Paraguay's farms and ranches. In 1926, a tornado nearly destroyed the city of Encarnación. A 1997 tornado caused the partial collapse of a stadium in Ciudad del Este, killing 33 people and injuring more than 200. Prolonged drought in the Chaco in 2002 caused 17 deaths.

Villa Hayes

Villa Hayes is a small city located to the north of Asunción. Oddly enough, it is named after U.S. president Rutherford B. Hayes. Hayes ruled in favor of Paraguay in a dispute between Paraguay and Argentina over claims to the Chaco region. This made Hayes a hero in Paraguay. Paraguay honored Hayes by changing the name of the city of Villa Occidental to Villa Hayes. Paraguay also renamed a department, which is a regional government similar to a state in the United States, Presidente Hayes.

Nature's Treasure Chest

Wildflowers growing in
the Chaco.

Paraguay has a huge mix of environments and climates. Parts of the country are located in the tropics, other regions are subtropical, and still another is semi-arid. Some parts of Paraguay receive heavy rain. Others experience devastating droughts. This variety of climates has created a complex web of plant and animal life.

The Magic Forests

When Europeans first arrived in eastern Paraguay, most of the land was covered in thick forests. The Guaraní Indians lived in the forests. Their language included many sounds that could be heard in the forests. The forest gave them life, and they worshipped nature. They had a concept of heaven, which they called *Yvaga*. Translated into English, *Yvaga* means "a place of abundant fruit trees." Early explorers noted that the Indians had names for more than a thousand species of plants. They also knew which plants could be used as medicines.

Plants and Animals of Paraguay

100,000 species of insects
8,000 to 12,000 species of plants
650 species of birds
250 species of fish
155 species of mammals
138 species of reptiles
69 species of amphibians

Opposite: **Ducks swim in a pond near Mariscal**

Paraguay's forests are being rapidly cut down to make room for farms.

The forests of eastern Paraguay are part of a vast region called the Interior Atlantic Forest. At one time, these forests covered more than 300 million acres (120 million hectares) in Brazil and Paraguay. Today, only about 7 percent of those forests remain. In Paraguay, they are located along the eastern border near Brazil and the southern border with Argentina. These forests are no longer in one continuous block. Instead, they are found in scattered fragments.

Vanishing Forests

Paraguay is losing its forests at a faster rate than any other country in South America. Most of the nation's forestland is owned by individuals rather than the government. These people are under heavy pressure to sell the land for farming. The trees are then cleared so crops can be planted. If Paraguay's forests continue to be cleared at current rates, they could disappear entirely in fifteen years. This would be a tragedy. Plants that contain valuable medicines might be lost forever. Endangered animals would simply disappear from the face of the earth. Without the trees to hold the soil in place, it would wash away. This would make the land less fertile, fill the lakes with silt, and pollute drinking water.

One of those fragments is the Mbaracayú Forest Nature Reserve, which is managed by the Moisés Bertoni Foundation. This protected forest contains hundreds of species of hardwood trees. One of those trees is the lapacho. The lapacho tree can reach a height of 100 feet (30 m) and can live 700 years. When the lapacho blossoms, its canopy explodes into vivid color. Some species have pink blossoms, while others are yellow, red, or violet. The forest floor is covered with a dense undergrowth of plants. It includes ferns that can grow several feet high.

A Healthy Tea

The native Indians of Paraguay harvested the inner bark of the lapacho tree to brew a special tea. The tea was rich in vitamins and minerals, and the Indians believed it helped them fight off disease.

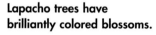

Lapacho trees have brilliantly colored blossoms.

The Sage of the Jungle

Moisés Bertoni was a Swiss botanist who settled in the Paraguayan jungle in 1887. He lived with his wife and thirteen children near the Río Paraná close to the Brazilian border until 1929. There, he studied the region's immense biodiveristy. With the help of his family, he collected and classified 7,000 different plant species. The Bertonis also classified more than 10,000 insects. The government of Paraguay has purchased Moisés Bertoni's 23,517 acres (9,517 ha) of land and declared it a protected national monument.

Wildlife

Paraguay's eastern forests are home to many animal species. Some of these creatures are in danger of becoming extinct. Among the endangered mammals that live in the forest are the jaguar, tapir, collared anteater, and white-lipped peccary. More than 420 different species of birds are common to these forests, including Paraguay's national bird, the bare-throated bellbird.

The National Flower

The *mburucuya* (passion fruit) is Paraguay's national flower. It is a vine that produces one of the most intricate and brightly colored blossoms in nature. The colors are delicate blues and lavenders, with a green starburst design in the center. The flower produces a tasty egg-sized fruit. The pulp can be squeezed to produce a refreshing, thirst-quenching juice, or it can be made into syrup or jelly.

The National Bird

The bare-throated bellbird is Paraguay's national bird. It is a shy bird seldom seen or photographed in the wild. But it is often heard. It has an extremely loud call that echoes through the forests of eastern Paraguay.

Many snakes can be found slithering through the undergrowth, including the anaconda and the fer-de-lance. The anaconda can reach lengths of up to 28 feet (8 m). Anacondas eat fish, deer, other snakes, and sometimes even jaguars. The anaconda squeezes its victim to death and then swallows it whole. The fer-de-lance is much smaller than the anaconda, generally about 6 feet (2 m) long, but it is much more dangerous to humans. That is because it is highly poisonous, and it lives in areas where there are people. Paraguayans have nicknamed the fer-de-lance *cinco minutos*, which means "five minutes." That is because someone who is bitten by a fer-de-lance will usually die within five minutes.

Anacondas are the world's biggest snakes. Pythons from Asia sometimes grow longer, but anacondas are much bigger around.

Caimans can grow up to 10 feet (3 m) long.

Grasslands

The natural grasslands of eastern Paraguay are the heartland of the nation's agriculture. They are located between Asunción and the forest belt. Large stretches of natural grasslands are used to graze livestock. Farmers have converted some of the grasslands to cropland for growing soybeans, corn, cassava, fruit, and other foods.

A Safe Haven

The Chaco is totally different from eastern Paraguay. The floods, droughts, scorching temperatures, salty soils, high winds, thorny bushes, poisonous snakes, and swarming insects make the Chaco a difficult environment.

An old Indian legend tells a story of the animals talking to God. They complained to God that there was no place for them to live without being harassed and killed by humans. God said he would send them to a safe place away from humans. According to the legend, he sent them to the Chaco. The Chaco is one of the safest places on earth for animals.

The word *Chaco* is derived from the Quechua Indian language. It means "great hunting ground." The Chaco is one of the last great retreats for big cats like the jaguar and the puma. It is also home to the endangered giant ant-bears and the maned wolf. The Chaco's swampy areas are teeming with caiman, capybara (the world's largest rodent), and hundreds of bird species.

Scientists estimate that about 5,000 giant peccaries live in the hot, dry Chaco.

Nature's Surprises

In 1972, scientists discovered live specimens of the world's largest peccary, a piglike animal. These creatures, which Paraguayans call *taguas*, weigh between 60 and 90 pounds (27 and 40 kg). Taguas forage during the night, eating mostly cactus. The discovery of living taguas surprised many scientists. Only their fossilized bones had been previously studied, and they had been declared extinct many years earlier.

Rivers in the Chaco dry up during long periods of drought. Yet one kind of fish can survive for months in these dry riverbeds. This is the lungfish, an ancient species of fish that has been on Earth for 350 million to 400 million years. A lungfish is about 4 feet (1.2 m) long and is shaped like an eel. When the dry season arrives, the fish buries itself in the mud and curls into a ball. It then secretes mucus, which hardens to form a cocoon around the lungfish. When the rains return, it uncurls and again begins swimming in the water.

Lungfish can grow up to 6 feet (2 m) long.

Plants in the Chaco

A tree has to be tough to survive in the Chaco. Still, more than 500 species of trees have adapted to this harsh environment. In the eastern Chaco, trees may reach 50 feet (15 m) in height. But in the west, there is little rainfall, so most trees don't even reach 10 feet (3 m).

The most famous tree in the Chaco is the quebracho. There are several species of quebracho. The white quebracho is cut for firewood. Tannin, which is used to cure leather hides, is made from the red quebracho. For many years, tannin was Paraguay's most important export.

The lapacho is among the tallest trees in the Chaco.

The palo santo's sweet-smelling wood is used to make incense. Its fragrance is also used to give soap and other goods a pleasant smell.

The algarrobo tree produces an exquisite wood used to make furniture. The *palo santo* (holy wood) is the source of oil of guaiac, a fragrance used in soap. Palm trees are harvested for palm hearts, a popular food in Paraguay.

Disappearing forests are not as serious a problem in the Chaco as in eastern Paraguay. It is estimated that only 15 percent of the forests in the Chaco have been cut down. The Chaco has few roads for logging trucks. And because most people do not want to live in the Chaco, farmland is not in demand there.

The hyacinth macaw is the largest parrot in the world.

Wetlands

Wetlands are some of the most fragile—and important—ecosystems on Earth. Wetlands act as a sponge, soaking up water to prevent flooding. Wetlands also serve as a filter to remove pollutants.

During the rainy season, as much as 15 percent of Paraguay is covered by marshes and swamps. These wetlands have thick growths of marsh grass, reeds, and other water-loving plants. They provide some of the best wildlife habitat in the world. Storks, egrets, herons, and flamingos flourish in the swamps. River otters, bright blue-feathered macaws, and brilliantly colored butterflies abound.

Recently, Paraguay has begun to protect its natural environment. The country established its first national park in 1965. In the past forty years, the people of Paraguay have set aside 3,462,284 acres (1,401,137 ha) of protected areas. Paraguay has twelve national parks, three national monuments, two biological refuges, two biological reserves, and one national reserve. Paraguay is becoming increasingly committed to preserving its national treasures.

Paraguay's rain forests are home to an incredible range of plant and animal life.

CHAPTER FOUR

History's Footprints

ATIVE INDIANS HAVE LIVED IN PARAGUAY FOR SEVERAL thousand years. They are believed to have entered the region between 8,000 and 9,000 years ago. Unfortunately, the ancient people left little evidence of their way of life. Almost all that remains from before Europeans arrived are pictures carved on rocks and cave walls. The ancient people carved images of geometric shapes, grid patterns, and animals such as the armadillo.

Opposite: **Ancient petro-glyph, Cerro Akua Hills**

Several different tribes lived in Paraguay long ago. They included the Guaraní, the Aché-Guayaki, the Toba-Maskoy, the Guaycurú, and the Payagúa.

The Guaraní lived in the forests of eastern Paraguay. They practiced slash-and-burn agriculture. This involved cutting a large patch of trees and burning the trunks, branches, and leaves. The ashes were spread across the clearing because it made the soil more fertile. The Guaraní planted corn, beans, manioc (cassava), pota-toes, bananas, and papaya. Wild

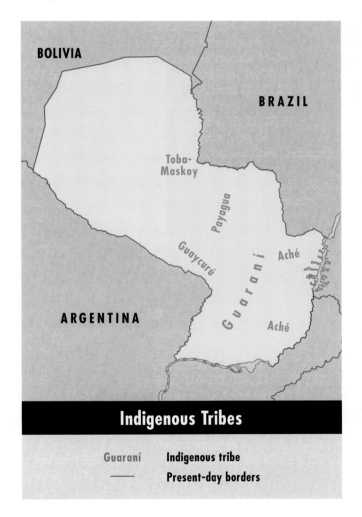

Indigenous Tribes

Guaraní   **Indigenous tribe**
——   **Present-day borders**

Long ago, many Paraguayan Indians lived in houses with thatched roofs.

game, fish, and several varieties of wild fruit were also important to the diet of the Guaraní.

The Guaraní lived in small settlements. They built houses using beams and poles cut from the trees. The houses had thatched roofs. One large house might be home to ten to fifteen families. Inside the houses, dividing walls separated the families. In each settlement, the houses were arranged around a central plaza.

A group of council chiefs governed each settlement. The chiefs were elders who represented the major families. Decisions were made by agreement of the majority of the council. Sometimes important decisions were influenced by a powerful shaman, or priest.

Life for the people of the Chaco, like the Guaycurú and Payaguá, was much more difficult. They did not farm. Instead, they were hunters and gatherers who were always on the move. Their survival depended on excellent tracking and hunting skills and knowing where to find water. They ate insects, reptiles, mammals, fish, birds, and other available foods. Chaco tribes were small. Most were hostile to any outsider who invaded their territory.

Invaders

Alejo García, the first European to visit Paraguay, had little interest in the region. He was a Portuguese explorer who had survived a shipwreck along the southeast coast of Brazil in 1516. He had heard rumors of incredible riches in a mountain kingdom to the west. After eight years of planning, he departed with a small group of Europeans for the kingdom of the Incas in the Andes Mountains.

In 1524, he crossed the Río Paraná and moved on to the Río Paraguay. As he traveled, he gathered an army of about 2,000 Guaraní warriors. They continued westward through the dangerous Chaco region and into the land of the Incas. The group attacked Inca settlements and took their silver. Finally, the Incas managed to drive the invaders out of their empire.

Incan warriors, shown here, drove off the Spaniards in 1524.

Sebastian Cabot spent three years exploring Paraguay.

Juan de Salazar de Espinosa founded Asunción in 1537.

During the return trip through Paraguay, García's Guaraní warriors turned on the Europeans. They murdered the entire group and kept the silver loot for themselves. But news of García's raid on the Incas increased Spain's interest in the region.

In 1526, Sebastian Cabot, an Englishman working for Spain, began a three-year journey of exploration on the Río Paraná and the Río Paraguay. He returned to Spain and reported to King Charles V that the region might have great riches. Spain officially claimed Paraguay as its own in 1535.

One year later, Spain sent eleven ships and 2,500 men to South America. Their goal was to find a route from Paraguay to the riches of Peru. Three of the ships sailed up the Río Paraguay. The commanders of these ships were experienced explorers named Juan de Ayolas, Domingo Martínez de Irala, and Juan de Salazar de Espinosa. They sailed far to the north of Paraguay where they anchored at present-day Fuerte Olimpo. Ayolas ventured into the Chaco and was never heard from again.

While Irala lingered in northern Paraguay, Salazar returned south down the river. On August 15, 1537, Salazar anchored his boat at a good site along the shoreline. August 15 was a religious holiday known as the Assumption of Mary. Salazar named the spot Nuestra Señora Santa María de la Asunción in honor of this holiday. Today, it is known simply as Asunción.

Domingo Martínez de Irala, the first governor of Paraguay, ruled for nearly twenty years.

The Spanish explorers, who were known as *conquistadores* (conquerors) mixed freely with the Guaraní Indians. Most of the Spaniards had children with several different Indian women. Irala is said to have produced more than 100 offspring. Within twenty years, the Spanish explorers had added more than 6,000 children to the local population. The Spaniards adopted many of the Guaraní customs and learned their language. These early events laid the foundation for Paraguay's mestizo population.

Asunción started out as a fort. It grew more important as silver was shipped from the Andes through the city and on to Europe. Asunción became the center of a Spanish province that covered much of southern South America. Irala was the first governor in the Americas who was elected by a vote of the colonists. He ruled from 1537 until his death in 1557, except for a short period of rule by Álvar Núñez Cabeza de Vaca. During his rule, Irala oversaw the construction of churches and public buildings and

Álvar Núñez Cabeza de Vaca

Álvar Núñez Cabeza de Vaca was an extraordinary explorer who sailed from Spain to North America in 1527. In 1528, his ship was destroyed in a hurricane off the coast of Florida. He and fellow survivors built rafts and reached Galveston Island in present-day Texas. From there, Cabeza de Vaca walked across the continent to the west coast of Mexico. It took him eight years. His story of survival in a hostile land is one of the great tales of all time. Cabeza de Vaca returned to Spain in 1537.

In 1540, Cabeza de Vaca sailed to Paraguay where he was appointed governor of the Spanish settlement at Asunción. He was appalled at how the colonists treated

the Indians. He tried to make changes. This angered the settlers. They threw him out of office, drummed up false charges against him, and sent him back to Spain to stand trial where he was found guilty. Cabeza de Vaca's adventures in the Americas were over.

the establishment of new settlements. The native population was forced to work on the *encomiendas*, large farms and ranches operated by the colonists.

A Perfect World

By the late 1500s, Jesuit priests had begun to arrive in Paraguay. Their mission was to convert the Guaraní Indians to Roman Catholicism. The Jesuits conducted most of their work in southeastern Paraguay. They established mission settlements known as *reducciones*. The first Paraguayan reducción was established in 1610. Over the next century, the Jesuits established thirty reducciones in Paraguay.

Each reducción had the same plan. The heart of the community was the village square. The church dominated one side of the square, towering above the other buildings. Indians who had converted to Catholicism lived in houses that faced outward on the other three sides of the square. The houses were large. Much like traditional Guaraní houses, they were divided into individual units for each family. The village also included a hospital, stables, priests' quarters, a school, crafts workshops, and sometimes an astronomical observatory. Sheep grazed in the large grassy space in the center of the square.

The Guaraní were willing converts to Catholicism. The reducciones saved them from Brazilian slave hunters and the harsh life on the encomiendas—where they were treated poorly by the owners.

The reducciones were almost completely self-sufficient. The workers raised the crops and livestock they needed for food. They grew their own cotton and made all of their own clothing. They had printing presses and published their own schoolbooks. Nearly every citizen could read and write. About the only products that the reducciones had to import were glass and paper.

The king of Spain forced the Jesuits to leave Paraguay in 1767. Their missions soon became ruins.

Other Spanish colonists were jealous of the Jesuit communities. They complained that the reducciones took all of the good workers. They were angry that the Jesuits did not pay taxes and that the Church was becoming wealthy. They suggested to Spanish authorities that the Jesuits might try to form an independent state. This aroused the attention of the

Paraguay's Greatest Missions

In 1993, the Jesuit Reducciones of La Santísima Trinidad de Paraná and Jesus de Tavarangue were named World Heritage Sites by the United Nation's Educational, Scientific and Cultural Organization (UNESCO). World Heritage Sites are places UNESCO has identified as being of unusual and irreplaceable importance to the history of mankind.

The government of Paraguay has been working to restore its missions to attract tourists. The crown jewel of the missions is the basilica at La Santísima Trinidad de Paraná, which was designed by the renowned Italian architect Gianbattista Primoli. The basilica took forty years to build and could seat 5,000 Guaraní worshippers.

Spanish king. In 1767, King Charles III kicked the Jesuits out of all Spanish territory. Within a few years, the reducciones lay in ruins, and many of the Guaraní had returned to the forests.

Change on the Horizon

During the Jesuit period, Asunción gradually declined in political power. It was governed from Lima as a part of the Spanish Viceroyalty of Peru. In reality, Buenos Aires, Argentina, had become the political center of the region. In 1776, Spain made Paraguay a part of the Viceroyalty of La Plata. Buenos Aires was named the capital of this viceroyalty.

Paraguayans were unhappy with this arrangement. The thought of taking orders from Buenos Aires was more than they could bear. In addition, Spain had imposed high taxes, so much of Paraguay's wealth was going overseas. By 1811, the Paraguayans had tired of Spanish control. On May 14, 1811, an uprising began. Its aim was to rid the country of Spanish rule. The uprising continued through May 15, which is now

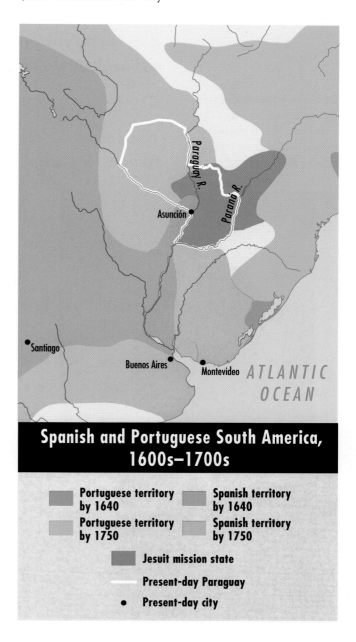

Spanish and Portuguese South America, 1600s–1700s

	Portuguese territory by 1640		Spanish territory by 1640
	Portuguese territory by 1750		Spanish territory by 1750
	Jesuit mission state		
—	Present-day Paraguay		
●	Present-day city		

celebrated as Paraguayan Independence Day. After nearly 300 years of Spanish rule, Paraguay was finally free to govern itself.

But self-rule would be a rough road. Paraguayans were about to embark on a political journey filled with instability and harsh dictatorships.

Dr. José Gaspar Rodríguez de Francia, Paraguay's first president, had a powerful personality and was popular among the poor.

The Supreme One

The first of the dictators was Dr. José Gaspar Rodríguez de Francia. He became the head of the government in 1814. Two years later, the National Assembly made him dictator for life. He ruled Paraguay with an iron fist and earned the nickname the Supreme One. His philosophy was that people would give up personal freedoms for an orderly, self-sufficient society. He enforced this philosophy.

Francia closed the country's borders, isolating the nation. He shut down the colleges, the post office, and all of the newspapers. He seized the Catholic Church's property and turned religious buildings into military housing. Anyone who looked at the presidential palace was to be shot immediately. Francia organized a secret police force to spy on his opponents. Several were jailed for life. Others were stabbed as he watched from his office window.

Despite all this, Francia did some good. He introduced modern methods of farming. He organized the military. And under his leadership, Paraguayans developed a sense of unity and independence.

The López Family

After Francia died in 1840, Carlos Antonio López began a twenty-two-year rule. López had strong dictatorial powers, but he ended many of Francia's policies. The borders were opened and trade increased. Industrialization was encouraged, and slavery was ended. Colleges were reopened, and some personal freedoms were restored.

Carlos Antonio López worked hard to end Paraguay's isolation from the rest of the world.

After Carlos Antonio's death, his son Francisco Solano López was elected president with dictatorial powers. Francisco was a large man with an even larger ego. In 1864, he went to war with Brazil because he was annoyed that Brazil was interfering with politics in the neighboring country of Uruguay. When Argentina refused to let Paraguayan troops pass through their country, he attacked Argentina. Later in 1864, Uruguay joined the war on the side of Brazil and Argentina. It became known as the War of the Triple Alliance. It was the bloodiest conflict in the history of Latin America.

The war ended in 1870 when López was killed. Paraguay lost 55,000 square miles (140,000 sq km) of territory during

Bolivian soldiers patrol during the Chaco War.

the war. The loss of life was almost beyond belief. Before the war, Paraguay was home to about 525,000 people. After the war, only 221,000 remained. And only about 15 percent of the people who survived were men.

Political Instability

From 1870 to 1932, various political groups tried to gain control of the government. During this period, Paraguay had more than thirty different presidents.

In 1932, Paraguay entered into another costly war, this time with Bolivia. Both countries claimed vast areas in the Chaco, where the border was poorly defined. Neither side would give up their claims to the land because it was thought oil and gas might be found in the region.

It was another bloody war. Bolivian Indians from cooler regions were not suited to fight in the heat and thorny scrub of the Chaco. The Bolivian death toll reached more than 50,000. The Paraguayans lost 36,000. More soldiers died of disease and thirst than from their wounds.

The Bolivians had more men and better equipment than the Paraguayans. But the Paraguayans fought brilliantly. In the end, Bolivia signed a peace treaty, giving up most of its claims to the Paraguayan Chaco.

After the Chaco War, a series of war heroes ruled Paraguay. Then in 1954, General Alfredo Stroessner took control of the government. He had the backing of the army and the Colorado Party, one of Paraguay's two major parties. Although

General Alfredo Stroessner ruled Paraguay for thirty-five years.

In 1989, General Andres Rodríguez overthrew Stroessner and took control of the government.

Paraguay's constitution at the time limited leaders to two terms in office, Stroessner was elected eight times. He ruled Paraguay for thirty-five years.

Stroessner used the military and the police to silence any challengers. Many of his opponents were tortured or killed. He kept other military officers happy by allowing them to grow wealthy from bribes, smuggling, fraud, and corruption. Yet he did have some accomplishments. Under his rule, inflation was curbed and the economy improved. He also attracted some foreign aid and built new schools.

In 1989, Stroessner's lengthy dictatorship came to an end. The military overthrew him and replaced him with General Andres Rodríguez. Rodríguez surprised many people by allowing open elections three months later. He easily won the election as president. He immediately changed some of Stroessner's harsh rules. Rodríguez eased restrictions on free speech and the right to assemble. Labor unions were allowed to operate, and political parties gained new freedoms.

The movement toward a more democratic government continued in 1993 with the election of Juan Carlos Wasmosy, who was not a military leader. He was followed in office five years later by Raúl Cubas Grau, who resigned his presidency just one year after being elected. He was accused of being involved in the assassination of his vice president, Luis María Argaña. In 2003, Nicanor Duarte Frutos was elected president. Today, Paraguayans are hopeful that the country can move forward, in peace.

Nicanor Duarte Frutos became president of Paraguay in 2003 after promising to decrease corruption in the country.

The Struggle for Democracy

During the nearly 300 years of Spanish colonial rule, Paraguayans were largely uneducated and isolated. They had little exposure to the outside world and knew little about how to participate in their own government. After independence in 1811, they were looking for leadership that would protect them in a hostile world—and that's why they've been dominated by powerful dictators ever since.

Paraguayans found a strong leader in Gaspar Rodríguez de Francia in 1814. He set the tone as to how the nation would be governed. He built a strong military that gave Paraguayans

Opposite: **The Presidential Palace, Asunción**

The National Flag

The Paraguayan flag has three equal horizontal bands of red, white, and blue. The Paraguayan flag is similar to the French flag, which was an international symbol of liberty at the time the Paraguayan flag was adopted. On the flag of Paraguay, the red stands for patriotism, courage, heroism, equality, and justice. White represents purity, firmness, union, and peace. The blue stripe symbolizes tranquility, love, knowledge, truth, and liberty.

Paraguay is the only member of the United Nations with a flag that has different emblems on each side. The emblems are located in the center of the white band. The national coat of arms is on one side. It shows a yellow, five-pointed star inside a green wreath.

Across the top are the words REPÚBLICA DEL PARAGUAY. The opposite side of the flag bears the Seal of the Treasury. It contains a yellow lion below a red cap of liberty and the words *Paz y Justicia* ("Peace and Justice").

a sense of security. They gave up many personal rights in exchange for this peace of mind. They lived for more than twenty-five years under Francia's unyielding control.

The foundation for dictatorial power in Paraguay was thus established. Over the next 175 years, Paraguay would be governed by leaders who had little respect for individual freedoms.

The last great dictator in Paraguay lost power in 1989. Since then, Paraguay has been inching toward a new future, with greater freedoms for all Paraguayans.

The 1992 Constitution

After many years of dictatorship, Paraguay is slowly moving toward democracy.

Paraguay has had several different constitutions since it became independent from Spain. All but one favored a highly centralized government that put control in the hands of the president. But the most recent constitution, from 1992, changed this. This new constitution spread power among many different groups.

The constitution added the office of vice president. The legislative branch of government was given new powers that balanced the powers of the president. The judicial branch also underwent important changes.

In Paraguay, everyone over age eighteen can vote.

The Supreme Court of Justice grew from five to nine members. The court was given the power to decide whether new laws were legal under the constitution. Decisions in the Supreme Court of Justice could not be appealed.

The 1992 constitution encouraged Paraguay to become more open and democratic. The constitution guarantees the vote for everyone over the age of eighteen. It guarantees Paraguayans the right to live where they want, travel where they want, and say what they want. The constitution gives Paraguayans the right to privacy. It protects freedom of the press. People have the right to gather and demonstrate peacefully. The constitution guarantees freedom of religion and the

NATIONAL GOVERNMENT OF PARAGUAY

Executive Branch

- PRESIDENT
- VICE PRESIDENT
- COUNCIL OF MINISTERS

Legislative Branch

- CHAMBER OF SENATORS (45 MEMBERS)
- CHAMBER OF DEPUTIES (80 MEMBERS)

Judicial Branch

- SUPREME COUNCIL OF JUSTICE
- COURTS OF APPEAL
- COURTS OF FIRST INSTANCE

right to join any political party or movement. It abolished the death penalty and gave native people the right to preserve their ethnic identity.

When the 1992 constitution was approved, people around Paraguay and the world saw it as a blueprint for democracy.

Executive Branch

Paraguay is a constitutional republic. The executive branch of government is made up of the president, the vice president, and the Council of Ministers. The president and vice president are each elected to one five-year term. A presidential candidate must be at least thirty-five years old and be Paraguayan by birth. Neither the president nor the vice president can run for reelection. No one who has served as president for more than twelve months may be elected vice president. The vice president can be elected president if he or she resigns his position six months before the election.

The president has many responsibilities. He or she signs bills into law and has the power to veto, or reject, laws. The president can nominate or remove government ministers. The president also directs foreign relations. The president may call special sessions of Congress, and he or she serves as commander-in-chief of the armed forces.

The Council of Ministers works closely with the president. The council serves as an advisory body to the president. The ministers discuss proposed laws and offer advice on them. Ministers must submit a written report of their activities to the president each year. This report is shared with the Congress.

Luis Castiglioni was elected vice president of Paraguay in 2003.

Legislative Branch

The National Congress is composed of two bodies. The Chamber of Senators has forty-five members, who are elected nationwide. The Chamber of Deputies has eighty members elected from the country's political departments, which are like provinces or states. Both senators and deputies are elected

Members of Paraguay's National Congress pass laws and approve budgets.

for five-year terms and can be reelected. Senators must be thirty-five years old and be native-born Paraguayans. Deputies must also be native-born Paraguayans but may be elected at age twenty-five.

The main duty of the Congress is to pass laws. It must also approve the annual budget. It can reject treaties and international agreements signed by the president. Congress was provided with a powerful tool to balance the authority of the president. It has the ability to impeach the president if he or she violates the Constitution.

The Congress can also censure, or condemn, public officials and recommend to the president that they be removed from office.

New members of Paraguay's Supreme Court are sworn in.

Judicial Branch

The highest court in the land is the Supreme Court of Justice. Supreme Court judges are appointed by the senate and the president. They must be at least thirty-five years old and be native-born Paraguayans. They must hold a doctor of law degree and have proven good character. They must also have a minimum ten years of experience as a lawyer, judge, or university law professor.

Supreme Court judges are appointed for an initial five-year term. At the end of this term, they must be confirmed. Then they serve another five-year term. If they are confirmed after the second term, they can only be removed from office if they are impeached. But Supreme Court judges must step down when they reach the age of seventy-five.

Paraguay's National Anthem

Paraguay's national anthem, *"Paraguayos, Républica o muerte!"* (Paraguayans, The Republic or Death!), was adopted in 1846. The words are by Francisco Esteban Acuña de Figueroa, and the music is by Francisco José Debali.

Spanish lyrics

A los pueblos de América in fausto,
Tres centurias un cetro oprimió,
Más un día soberbia surgiendo,
Basta!, dijo y el cetro rompió.
Nuestros padres lidiando grandiosos,
Ilustraron su gloria marcial;
Y trozada la augusta diadema,
Enalzaron el gorro triunfal,
Y trozada la augusta diadema,
Enalzaron el gorro triunfal.

CHORUS:

Paraguayos, República o muerte!
Nuestro brío nos dío libertad;
Ni opresores, ni siervos, alientan,
Donde reinan unión, e igualdad.
Ni opresores, ni siervos, alientan,
Donde reinan unión e igualdad,
unión e igualdad, unión e igualdad.

English lyrics

For three centuries a reign oppressed
The unhappy peoples of America,
But one day, their anger aroused, they said:
"An end to this!" and broke the reign.
Our forefathers, fighting magnificently,
Displayed their martial glory,
And when the august diadem was shattered,
They raised the triumphal cap of liberty.

CHORUS:

Paraguayans, Republic or death!
It was our strength that gave us our final liberty.
Neither tyrants nor slaves can continue,
Where unity and equality reign,
Where unity and equality reign.

The main responsibility of the judicial branch is to interpret and enforce the constitution. The Supreme Court has the power to declare laws unconstitutional.

Most cases in Paraguay are tried in Courts of First Instance. Rulings in these courts can be questioned in the Courts of Appeal. These courts' rulings can be appealed to the Supreme Court. Supreme Court rulings cannot be appealed.

Regional Government

Paraguay is divided into seventeen political units. These units are called departments. Each department is administered by a governor who is elected by the people living in that department. Governors serve five-year terms.

Political Parties

The two most prominent political parties in Paraguay are the Colorados and the Liberals. Party membership has little to do with political beliefs. Belonging to a party is more about absolute loyalty to the party's candidates. Sometimes, this loyalty is rewarded with jobs. Family history usually determines which party a person belongs to. A person who changes political parties is considered a traitor to the family.

International Relations

Throughout much of its history, Paraguay has been isolated from other countries. This was the result of both Paraguay's location and the decisions of its political leaders. The country has gone to war with each of its neighbors at least once.

Paraguay's first powerful dictator, Gaspar Rodríguez de Francia, withdrew the nation from international contact. In the twentieth century, General Alfredo Stroessner insulted the international community by providing a haven for war criminals and fallen dictators.

Since dictator Alfredo Stroessner left power in 1989, Paraguay has improved its relations with other countries.

But the international community has begun to warm up to Paraguay in recent years. The 1992 constitution has provided great hope for change in Paraguay. As a result, the nation is more widely accepted around the globe. Paraguay is a member of the United Nations, an organization including most of the world's nations that is dedicated to solving problems peacefully. The country is becoming more active in other international groups, such as the Organization of American States, the World Trade Organization, and the Río Group.

Military Power

In 2001, more than 18,600 young men were serving in Paraguay's armed forces. Military service is required for men. Young men can be drafted for service at the age of seventeen. Women do not serve in the military. Paraguayan fighters are known for being good in combat and are tough opponents.

Asunción: Did You Know This?

Asunción, the capital city of Paraguay, is built on low hills along the eastern bank of the Paraguay River. Its elevation is between 300 and 400 feet (90 and 120 m) above sea level. The city has an average January temperature of 82°F (27.8°C) and an average July temperature of 65°F (18.3°C).

Asunción was founded on August 15, 1537, by Spanish explorer Juan de Salazar. He named the city Our Lady Santa María of Asunción, in honor of a holiday dedicated to Mary, the mother of Jesus.

Today, the city is simply called Asunción. It is the largest city in Paraguay. About 1.5 million people live in the city and its suburbs.

Asunción is the political and financial center of Paraguay, as well as its most important port. One of Asunción's prized colonial buildings is the Casa de la Independencia, where Paraguay declared its independence in 1811. Other interesting buildings are the Presidential Palace, the Pantheon of Heroes, and the Metropolitan Cathedral, which dates to 1687.

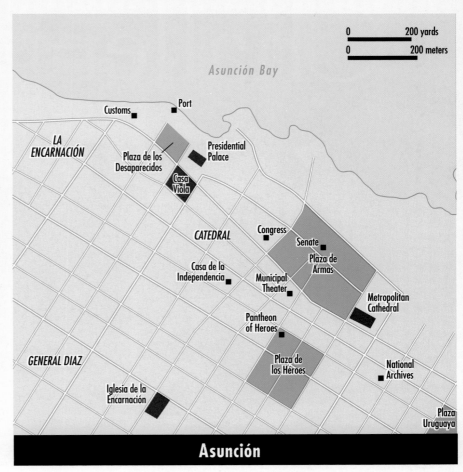

Asunción

Economic Challenges

P ARAGUAY HAS ALWAYS BEEN A POOR NATION. THE COUNTRY has almost no mineral resources. Its factories produce less than any other South American country. The nation's long history of political instability has discouraged foreign investment. And its location in the center of the continent has isolated it from global markets. Historically, Paraguay has depended heavily on agriculture. But now many Paraguayans hope that their nation will be able to rise to the economic challenges it faces and play a more active role in the global economy.

Opposite: **A farmer harvests sugarcane in San Pedro.**

Paraguay's Currency

The national currency of Paraguay is the Guaraní. The paper currency comes in denominations of 1,000, 5,000, 50,000, and 100,000. Paraguayan coins come in denominations of 1, 5, 10, 50, 100, and 500 Guaranís. One U.S. dollar equals 6,250 Guaranís.

Agriculture is the largest part of the Paraguayan economy.

The Heart of the Economy

Agriculture is at the heart of the Paraguayan economy. Nearly one-half the labor force works in agriculture. Most of the products that Paraguay exports to other countries are agricultural.

The Paranena region of eastern Paraguay is the center of Paraguayan agriculture. The soil there is fertile, and there is plenty of rainfall.

Two types of farming happen in Paraguay—subsistence and commercial. Subsistence farmers eat most of what they grow. They have little left over to sell. More than 200,000 families in Paraguay depend on subsistence farming for a livelihood. Most of their farms are located on public land, and the families seldom own their farm. The farms are small, averaging 25 acres (10 ha) in size.

The most common subsistence crop is cassava, a root vegetable that is central to the Paraguayan diet. Subsistence farmers also grow corn, beans, vegetables, and fruit and have a few head of livestock. They use oxen to plow their fields, and children are expected to help tend the crops and livestock.

In commercial farming, the crops are sold rather than eaten by the people who grow them. Commercial farms are large and mechanized. Soybeans are Paraguay's most important cash crop, followed by sugarcane and cotton. Many of the nation's largest farms have been purchased by Brazilian investors. In some cases, the government is forcing small farmers off public land and then selling the land to large commercial farms. This policy creates more exports for Paraguay, but it is devastating to the families who had been subsistence farmers.

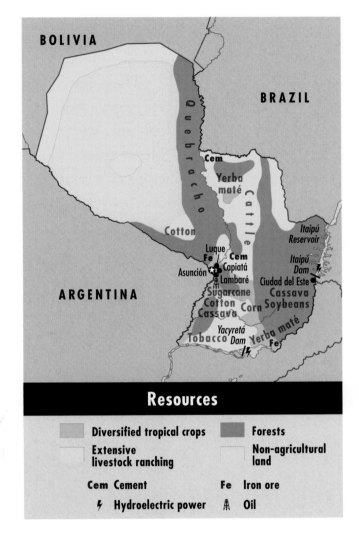

The Chaco, which covers 60 percent of the nation, is used primarily for ranching. Many of the ranches are very large. The Casado Ranch in the eastern Chaco once covered an area larger than Switzerland. Brahma, Zebu, and Santa Gertrudis are all popular breeds of cattle raised on the sprawling estates.

The Chaco produces less than 2 percent of all crops in Paraguay. Most of these crops are grown by Mennonite colonists who founded settlements in the central Chaco. The Mennonites built irrigation systems to bring water to their crops. Without these irrigation systems, the crops, the cattle, and the people could not survive in the Chaco.

About 8 million cattle are being raised in Paraguay.

Natural Resources

Forests are an important resource in Paraguay. In 2000, more than 124,131,054 cubic feet (3,515,000 cu m) of timber were cut for lumber. Most of this timber was tropical hardwoods from the eastern forests. Paraguay hardwoods are highly valued on the international market. The forests are also the major source of fuel for the country's citizens.

Some forests are being cleared to make new farmland. In fact, Paraguay has the highest rate of deforestation in South America. This is a major concern to environmentalists. If Paraguay's forests continue to be cut at the rate they have been, they could disappear entirely in fifteen years.

Mining is one of the least important economic activities in Paraguay. The country has few mineral resources. Even though the Chaco War with Bolivia was fought over potential oil and gas deposits, those deposits never came about. Currently, limestone, clay, sand, salt, and gypsum are mined in Paraguay.

Clay is one of Paraguay's leading mining products. It is used to make tiles and many other products.

What Paraguay Grows, Makes, and Mines

Agriculture (2000)

Cassava	4,400,000,000 metric tons
Soybeans	3,900,000,000 metric tons
Sugarcane	3,200,000,000 metric tons

Manufacturing (1996)

Portland cement	700,000 metric tons
Sugar	135,000 metric tons
Soya bean oil	126,400 metric tons

Mining (2000)

Lime	90,000 metric tons
Clay	66,500 metric tons
Sand	10,000 metric tons

Leather shoes and boots are among the few products manufactured in Paraguay.

Manufacturing

Paraguay does not do a lot of manufacturing. Manufacturing employs only about 10 percent of the country's workers. Most of Paraguay's manufacturing plants are small, and most process agricultural products. Cotton is used to manufacture textiles. Cattle hides are tanned and made into a wide range of leather products. Packing plants process beef for export. In 2001, Paraguay was approved as a beef producer for the European Union, an organization of most of the nations in Europe. This allowed Paraguay to export much more beef.

Harnessing Nature

Tapping Paraguay's powerful rivers as a source of energy and income has helped the nation's economy. Since the mid-1970s, Paraguay has joined Brazil and Argentina to build two of the largest hydroelectric projects in the world. In both cases, dams were built on the Paraná River. The water rushing downstream turns turbines in the dams, which produce electricity.

Turbines at Itaipú Dam

Facts About Itaipú

- The project was constructed from 1973 to 1991 at an estimated cost of $18 billion.
- The dam is 4.8 miles (7.7 km) long and 643 feet (196 m) high.
- The lake that formed behind the dam covers 870 square miles (2,253 sq km).
- During the peak period of construction, the project employed 40,000 workers.
- The steel used in the project would build 380 Eiffel Towers.
- The project used fifteen times more concrete than was used to build the tunnel under the English Channel.
- The project produces as much electricity as burning 434,000 barrels of oil a day.
- The site has attracted more than 11 million visitors since 1997.
- Paraguay's income from the project pays for 25 percent of the national budget.

Itaipú, a joint project with Brazil, is the second-largest hydroelectric facility on earth. Itaipú has a generating capacity of 12,600 megawatts. The Yacyretá project with Argentina has a capacity of 2,700 megawatts. Together, they take care of almost all of Paraguay's electrical needs. These two hydroelectric projects allow the country to export more than 90 percent of the electricity it generates. Paraguay is the largest exporter of electricity in Latin America.

Transportation and Communications

Paraguay's transportation system is poorly developed. Although Paraguay has 16,094 miles (25,901 km) of roads, only 1,906 miles (3,067 km) are paved. During the rainy season, many of the unpaved roads become impassable.

The nation has only one working railroad. It connects Asunción and Encarnación. The lack of railroads hurts

Paraguay's economy because it is difficult to move farm prod- **Docks on the Río Paraguay**
ucts. Meanwhile, only two airports in Paraguay handle
international flights.

River traffic is Paraguay's most important connection with
the global community. Asunción, Villeta, and Encarnación are
the major ports. Several Paraguayan and international ship-
ping companies operate on Paraguay's rivers, however, even
river traffic faces problems. During the dry season, river travel
is difficult. And during the rainy season, it can be dangerous.

People carry illegal goods into Brazil. The Ciudad del Este region is the center of smuggling in Paraguay.

Paraguay has the worst telephone network in South America. This scares off foreign investors. The country of Taiwan recently canceled a major project in Paraguay because of the poor telephone service.

Lingering Problems

Many nations around the world saw their economies develop rapidly over the past half-century. But Paraguay's economy was stagnant. Some of the blame can be laid at the feet of President Alfredo Stroessner, Paraguay's dictator for thirty-five years. For part of his rule, Paraguay's government was ranked as one of the three most corrupt governments in the world. Stroessner stayed in office by allowing his friends and military officers to gain great wealth through illegal activities.

Stroessner's friends helped political and military cronies build an underground economy that favored only a small portion of Paraguay's citizens. This economy included smuggling and the sale of illegal weapons and drugs. The center for this activity was in Ciudad del Este, along the Brazilian border. Cocaine from Bolivia and Peru moved across the border to Brazil's large cities. Marijuana grown in Paraguay was sold in many South American countries. Computers, TVs, cameras, liquor, and cigarettes were smuggled from Paraguay into Brazil. Over the years, many government officials grew wealthy by accepting bribes to ignore the lawbreakers.

Despite these troubles, hope is on the horizon. If Paraguay's fragile democracy is allowed to develop, positive changes will occur. An honest government will provide an economic climate that attracts foreign investors. New money flowing into the country will help improve Paraguay's transportation and communication systems. Paved highways, more rail service, a modern telecommunications network, and new technology could help move Paraguay into the twenty-first century.

Illegal drugs pour across the border into Brazil. Drugs that are seized are destroyed.

A Mix of Peoples

For much of Paraguay's history, one ethnic group dominated the country. Almost all Paraguayans were mestizo, people of both Spanish and Indian background. But in the last century, people have immigrated to Paraguay from around the world. Now, Paraguay's population is rising as it becomes a country with people from many backgrounds.

Opposite: **A rug seller in Asunción**

Population

In 2004, the population of Paraguay topped six million. For much of Paraguay's history, population growth was slow. During Spanish rule, few Europeans wanted to settle in Paraguay because of its remote location. After Paraguay became independent, its borders were closed and immigration was not allowed for more than thirty years. Two bloody wars killed many Paraguayans, cutting the population even further.

But in the past century, Paraguay has promoted immigration to help increase its population. Today,

Persons per square mile	Persons per square kilometer
65–130	25–50
25–64	10–24
3–24	1–9
fewer than 3	fewer than 1

Population of Paraguay's Largest Cities (2003)

Asunción	539,200
Ciudad del Este	223,400
San Lorenzo*	202,700
Luque*	170,400
Capiatá*	154,500
Lambare*	120,000
Fernado de la Mora*	114,300
Limpio*	71,700
Nemby*	71,300
Encarnación	69,800

*These cities are suburbs of Asunción

Paraguay's annual population growth rate of 2.5 percent is one of the highest rates on the continent.

Where Do People Live?

Paraguay's citizens are not equally distributed across the country. Ninety-seven percent of the population lives in the Parenena, the region east of the Paraguay River that includes just 40 percent of the nation's land area. Most Paraguayans live within 100 miles (160 km) of Asunción, the nation's capital and its largest city. In fact, seven of Paraguay's ten largest cities are suburbs of Asunción. The Asunción area now contains about 1.5 million people.

Asunción is home to twice as many people as any other city in Paraguay.

Few people live in the remote Chaco region.

Paraguay's second-largest city, Ciudad del Este, is home to more than 220,000 people. It is located along the Paraná River border with Brazil. The rest of the population of eastern Paraguay is scattered on farms or in small towns of less than 70,000 people.

Just 3 percent of Paraguayans live in the Chaco, the vast region west of the Paraguay River. The sparsely settled Chaco is home to a few military installations, large cattle ranches, Mennonite colonies, and some Indians. There are no major cities and hardly any paved roads.

Almost all Paraguayans have both Spanish and Indian ancestors.

Ethnic Composition

Mestizo	95%
Other: Brazilian, Indian, German, Asian, Arab, Italian, Spanish	5%

Land of the Mestizo

Ninety-five percent of all Paraguayans are mestizo. The early Spanish conquistadores arrived in Paraguay without their wives, and it was common for them to take Indian wives. The mixing of Spanish and Indian blood continued, and now almost all Paraguayans are mestizo. Paraguayans are proud of the Guaraní Indian history that gives them a distinct national identity.

The Immigrants

The War of the Triple Alliance (1864–1870) had a devastating effect on Paraguay's population. It is estimated that Paraguay had a population of 525,000 at the start of the war. By the time the war ended, only 221,000 survived. In the years that followed, the Paraguayan government invited foreigners to come and help rebuild the nation.

Between 1882 and 1907, about 12,000 immigrants arrived in Asunción. They came from Germany, Italy, Spain, France, and Argentina. In 1893, a group of 220 colonists arrived from Australia. The colonists wanted to establish a perfect community where everyone lived together in harmony, under the leadership of socialist William Lane. The colony, which was named Nueva Australia (New Australia), attracted a second group of settlers in 1894.

The War of the Triple Alliance in the mid-1800s killed more than half the people in Paraguay.

But Lane proved to be a poor leader. The colonists began arguing among themselves, and the Paraguayan government withdrew its support. Many of the settlers returned to Australia.

The Germans

In 1881, five German families arrived from Berlin. They established a small settlement, which they named New Bavaria. In later years, the name was changed to San Bernardino. Many German families still live in the area, which has become a popular tourist site for Asunción's wealthy families.

In 1887, Bernard Foster and his wife, Elizabeth, founded the colony of Nueva Germania. Elizabeth was the sister of the noted German philosopher Friedrich Nietzche. The Fosters were anti-Semitic, meaning they believed Jews were inferior. They thought northern Europeans were better than all other people on Earth. The Fosters dreamed of building a master race in Paraguay.

They had a large impact on the continuing stream of Germans arriving in Paraguay. A new German colony was established at Hohenau near Encarnación in 1899. As German immigration continued, several settlements were established west of the Paraná River. Another wave of German settlers arrived after World War II ended.

The German settlers had a major impact on political ideas in Paraguay. Adolf Hitler and his Nazi Party rose to power in Germany in the 1930s. The Nazis believed that the government should be powerful and that Jews were inferior. Their beliefs were echoed in the German communities in Paraguay.

Paraguay's German immigrants founded the first branch of the Nazi Party in South America in 1931. The German settlements proudly displayed swastikas, the symbol of the Nazis, and pictures of Hitler. In return for their loyalty, Hitler's government sent schoolbooks written in German, school uniforms, and boxes of swastika flags. In 1937, a law was passed prohibiting Jews from entering Paraguay.

Hitler believed Germany should dominate Europe, and he began invading one country after another. In 1939, World War II broke out. In subsequent years, people of many nationalities—including the British, Russians, and Americans—tried to stop him. Secretly, many Paraguayans favored Germany in the war. Paraguay did not declare war on Germany until three months before the war ended. By this time, the outcome was no longer in doubt. After the war, more than 300 Nazis fled to safety in Paraguay.

Many Germans who settled in Paraguay supported Adolf Hitler.

The Mennonites are the most successful farmers in the Chaco.

The Mennonites who arrived in Paraguay between the 1920s and 1940s also spoke German. But they arrived from Canada, the Ukraine, and eastern Siberia. They had previously fled Germany to escape religious persecution. Mennonites were not interested in politics. They just wanted to be left alone to practice their religion and raise their families. Paraguay had the perfect spot for them—the Chaco. The Paraguayan government wanted to establish settlements in the Chaco as a way of keeping Bolivians out of the region.

The Paraguayans and the Mennonites held lengthy discussions before the Mennonites agreed to come. The Mennonites demanded total religious freedom. They insisted that they not be forced to serve in the military. They wanted the right to operate their own schools in the German language. They would set up their own medical facilities and banks. Paraguay agreed to their demands and passed a law to protect these rights.

The first group of 2,000 Mennonites arrived from Canada in 1926 and 1927. They founded the Menno Colony. A second group, from the Ukraine and the Amur River area of Siberia, founded the Fernheim Colony in 1930. The final wave of Mennonites, who arrived from Russia in 1947, started the Neuland Colony.

Today, more than 30,000 Mennonites live in twenty different settlements in Paraguay. Filadelfia, in the central Chaco, is the cultural, commercial, and financial headquarters for the Mennonite community. The Mennonites stand out in Paraguay because of their fair skin, blonde hair, and blue eyes.

The Mennonites have proven to be some of Paraguay's most successful farmers and ranchers. A strong work ethic and stubborn sense of survival has allowed them to succeed in a very difficult environment. They grow sorghum, sesame, and peanuts on their farms. They also raise beef livestock and dairy cattle. The Mennonite colonies produce 70 percent of Paraguay's dairy products.

Asian Faces

The first Japanese settlement at La Colmena was established in 1936. Two more Japanese colonies were founded near Encarnación in the 1950s. Today, an estimated 12,000 people of Japanese descent live in Paraguay. Most work in agriculture. They specialize in raising fruits and vegetables as well as chickens and pigs.

In the beginning, the Japanese settlers wanted to maintain their own culture. They ran their own schools in which all classes were taught in Japanese. Eventually, this changed, and they started teaching classes in Guaraní and Spanish. Most Japanese children speak Japanese, Guaraní, and Spanish. By and large, the Japanese have not mixed with the mestizo population. There is a strong prejudice against Paraguayan–Japanese intermarriage.

An estimated 30,000 to 50,000 Koreans and ethnic Chinese have settled in Paraguay. Both groups are found primarily in Ciudad del Este and Asunción. Many are involved in importing and selling electronic goods made in Asia.

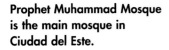

Prophet Muhammad Mosque is the main mosque in Ciudad del Este.

Arabs

Since the construction of the Itaipú hydroelectric plant, the population of Ciudad del Este has exploded. The city is located in the heart of an area called the Tri-Border region. This is located where Brazil, Argentina, and Paraguay meet. The area is home to an estimated 20,000 Middle Eastern immigrants. The largest numbers of Arabs arrived from Lebanon and Syria. Many Arabs are involved in the import and export trade.

Ciudad del Este is filled with stores that cater to Brazilians.

Brasiguayos

For many years, Paraguay had a law that prohibited foreigners from buying land within 93 miles (150 km) of the border. In 1967, this law was repealed. This opened the floodgates of immigration: Paraguay experienced the greatest influx of foreigners in the country's history.

During the 1970s, wealthy Brazilians could buy land in Paraguay at a price seven to eight times cheaper than comparable land in Brazil. They bought large tracts of land and cleared the forests. Then they subdivided the land into smaller units and sold them to Brazilian immigrants. The new immigrants were soon operating successful soybean farms. Many small Paraguayan farmers and Indians were evicted from their land so it could be sold to the Brazilians. Hard feelings linger.

Currently, between 350,000 and 400,000 Brazilians live in eastern Paraguay. The Paraguayans call the newcomers Brasiguayos. Like Brazilians, the Brasiguayos speak Portuguese, use Brazilian money, fly the flag of Brazil, and cheer for the Brazilian soccer team. Tensions between the Brasiguayos and the Paraguayans remain high.

The Native Americans

Today, Paraguay is home to seventeen different tribal groups. Their numbers are estimated to be between 50,000 and 75,000, but no one knows for sure. Many Indians in the Chaco have never been counted. More than half of the Indians live

The Maca Indians live in the Chaco.

in settlements run by missionary organizations. Others have tried to find work on ranches or in the Mennonite colonies.

Even though 95 percent of all Paraguayans have Indian blood in their veins, considerable prejudice exists. Many Paraguayans look down on the wandering tribes of the Chaco. The Indians are often discriminated against in jobs and are paid lower wages than other Paraguayans.

Two Tongues

Paraguay is officially a bilingual nation. The two languages are Spanish and Guaraní. Although Guaraní is spoken by many Paraguayans, it did not become an official language until 1992. Teaching Guaraní in primary and secondary schools became required in 1994.

Common Spanish and Guaraní Words and Phrases

Spanish	Guaraní	English
Adiós	Tereiko pora	Good-bye
Buenos días	Mba'e'ichapa ne ko'e	Good morning
Cuánto?	Mbovy'pa?	How much?
Dónde?	Mamo'pa?	Where?
Habla español?	Mezcla de espanol?	Do you speak Spanish?
Gracias	Aguyje	Thank you
No es posible	Ndikatu'i	It is not possible
Es muy sabroso?	Heve tisyrygui?	Does it taste good?
Grande	Guasu	Big

The Guaraní language uses many of the sounds of the rain forest. Some Guaraní words sound like what they mean. For example, *sununu* means "thunder," *piriri* means "to shiver," *pororo* means "popcorn," and *chororo* means "running water." The Guaraní language is often used in poems and songs.

Educated and upper-class people in Paraguay usually speak Spanish. Many parents want their children to speak Spanish so they can get ahead in business and appear to be well educated. Guaraní is more common in rural areas.

Nature, God, and Faith

R ELIGION IS WOVEN INTO THE SOCIAL FABRIC OF LIFE IN Paraguay. The original Guaraní natives believed in many gods. When Spanish priests arrived in the sixteenth century, many Indians converted to Catholicism. Today, 95 percent of all Paraguayans are Catholic. The other 5 percent are Protestant or follow religions brought to Paraguay by different ethnic groups. Before 1992, Catholicism was the official religion of Paraguay. The new constitution guaranteed freedom of religion, however, so Paraguay no longer has an official religion.

Opposite: **A church in Itagua**

The Guaraní Religion

The Guaraní Indians had a strong belief system when the Spanish arrived. They worshipped nature and believed that good spirits protected the plants and animals of the forest. Their main god was Tupa, who was the master of the universe. They believed that Tupa created all life. His home was the sun, and his wife was Arasy, the mother of heaven.

The ancient Guaraní had a story of how the world was created. They

A carving of Tupa at the Mythological Museum in Capiatá

believed that one day long ago, Tupa and Arasy visited Earth. They arrived on a hilltop near Areguá, Paraguay. Here they created the seas, rivers, forests, stars, and all living animals. Then Tupa created the first human couple in his likeness. He used clay, the juices of a special weed, and the blood of a night bird. Then he added the leaves of other plants and one centipede. Tupa soaked this mixture with water from a nearby spring named Tupakua, or the "fountain of God." This spring is well known in Paraguay because it is the source of Lake Ypakarai. Tupa set the two statues in the sun to dry and then gave them life.

The male was given the name Rupave, and the female was called Sypave. They were told they would be the father and mother of a new race. Tupa gave the new couple advice on how to live. He gave them all the products of the earth to use, but he cautioned them that they must not waste these resources. Tupa also told them that life on Earth was not final.

Beware the Night

The Guaraní who lived in the forests faced many real dangers. Jaguars and puma were a threat. The forest was home to snakes that could crush the life out of a body. Other snakes could inject venom that brought death in less than five minutes. Because of such creatures, people had a fear and respect of the dark. Alone in the jungle, a person's imagination could create images of unseen monsters.

Some of those imagined monsters became part of Guaraní mythology. Many were animals and others had human characteristics. Mboya-jagwa was a huge dog-snake that ate travelers and barked like a puppy. Carbúnculo was an ugly meat-eating hog that disguised himself as a water trough and gobbled up unsuspecting drinkers.

Kurupi was a man-figure so ugly that he inspired terror in everyone's heart. He could be invisible if he chose to be, but his bad breath gave him away. Even today, rural mestizos leave gifts of alcohol and tobacco on the back porch for Kurupi. They believe he guards their fields and animals, and they do not want to offend him.

Chaco Legends

The legends of the people of the Chaco almost always involve animals. Birds, alligators, anteaters, jaguars, and foxes are key characters. The favorite animal is the fox, who likes to pull pranks.

According to local beliefs, the fox is responsible for the fish in the rivers. Long ago, a fox approached the bottle tree that contained all of the water and fish in the world. The fox stole the key to a door in the bottle tree's trunk. When he opened the door, all the waters of the world rushed out and caused a great flood. The poor fox was drowned. But when the water withdrew, the rivers were full of fish.

He shared with the new couple a glimpse of the future. He told them that one day a man from another continent would arrive and control the destiny of the Guaraní.

Rupave and Sypave had three sons and many daughters. These children became the spirit gods of the Guaraní. The Guaraní believed that they were the descendants of Rupave and Sypave. Their faith required them to live in harmony with nature.

The Guaraní belief that someone would arrive from another continent seemed to be fulfilled when the Spanish arrived. The Catholic priests told the Guaraní a story of creation that was similar to the Indians' own beliefs. The Guaraní soon adopted Catholic saints as spirit gods. The two religions mixed comfortably, though the Guaraní kept many of their myths and folklore.

The Roman Catholic Church

Catholicism is the dominant religion in Paraguay. The first Catholic bishop arrived in Asunción in 1556. In 1588, three Jesuit missionaries arrived. For more than a century and a half, the Jesuits converted Indians to Christianity. The Jesuits accomplished this while protecting the Indians in settlements called reducciones. In 1767, the Spaniards kicked the Jesuits out of Paraguay. The king of Spain believed that the wealth and power of the Jesuits was a threat to his authority.

After the Jesuits left Paraguay, the Catholic Church lost much of its influence there. Independence from Spain in 1811 did not change that. Paraguay's first dictator, José Gaspar

Churches are prominent throughout Paraguay.

Rodríguez de Francia, cut off all communication with the head of the Roman Catholic Church. During the War of the Triple Alliance, Francisco Solano López had the Bishop of Asunción executed. By the time the war ended in 1870, only fifty-five priests were left in the entire country. No strong religious leaders had survived.

But over time, the Paraguayan government made peace with the Catholic Church. A new constitution in 1940 made Roman Catholicism the official state religion.

During the Stroessner dictatorship, from 1954 to 1989, church leaders started speaking out against the government. They openly criticized Stroessner's abuses of the Paraguayan people, particularly the poor. Priests delivered sermons demanding political freedom and social justice. Students at Catholic University in Asunción held demonstrations against the government. Stroessner's government responded by kicking vocal foreign priests out of the country. Protesting students were beaten, arrested, and tortured. But the Church did not back down. It remained a strong voice in support of people's rights.

The Stroessner government was ousted in 1989. The Catholic Church had played an important part in the fall of the dictatorship.

In 1992, the Catholic Church took a new position regarding its relationship with the government. The Church asked that it be dropped as Paraguay's official religion. The 1992 constitution established a separation of church and state. It also guaranteed religious freedom to all.

Major Religions

Roman Catholic	95%
Protestant	3%
Other religions	2%

Religion plays an important role in the social life of Catholic Paraguayans. Crosses dangle from the mirrors of buses and taxis. The Virgin Mary, the mother of Jesus, is especially adored in Paraguay, and her image is everywhere. Most homes display pictures of saints and have a small family shrine. Church rituals identify important stages in each person's life. Baptism, confirmation, marriage, last rights, and burial services are all significant events.

Women play a much more active role in the church in Paraguay than men do. Society demands that women be more devout. They are expected to go to church, and they are much more likely to pray. Men, on the other hand, are not expected to be overly concerned about religion. Many only go to church on holidays. Oftentimes, men can be found standing at the back of the church, ready for a quick exit.

Rituals such as weddings are central to Paraguayan life.

The Virgin of Caacupé

Caacupé is the capital of the Department of Cordillera. It is also the religious capital of Paraguay and the country's most important holy site. The center of the city is dominated by the cathedral called Nuestra Señora de los Milagros (Our Lady of Miracles).

December 8 is Virgin of Caacupé Day, Paraguay's most important religious holiday. Each year, hundreds of thousands of pilgrims converge on Caacupé to celebrate a mass to honor the Virgin Mary. The mass lasts all day and sometimes all night. Some pilgrims walk all the way across Paraguay to prove their devotion. They sleep on straw mats on sidewalks, plazas, and parks. For many of the faithful, this holiday is more important than Christmas.

Mennonite communities are thriving in the Chaco.

Mennonites

The Mennonites are the second-largest religious group in Paraguay, with more than 30,000 followers. They came to Paraguay to escape religious persecution. Religion is the foundation of Mennonite communities. They work hard on their farms and ranches six days a week. They believe that idleness is the devil's workshop. On Sunday, all activity comes to a standstill so they can worship together as a community.

Part of being a good Mennonite means preaching the gospel to nonbelievers. Thousands of Chaco Indians have accepted Mennonite religious teachings and have been baptized. Mennonites also believe that they must do good for others. They operate medical clinics for the ill and day care centers for needy parents. In Capiatá, they sponsor a retirement home for the aged. Most of the Mennonites who work at these places are young volunteers committed to their beliefs.

The Anglican church has been active in Paraguay since 1850. The first Anglicans in the country were British engineers who came to help build the railways. Their numbers increased after 1912 when Saint Andrews Church of Asunción was founded. The Anglican church in Paraguay now has one English-speaking parish in Asunción and more than thirty Spanish-speaking parishes. There are between 8,000 and 10,000 Anglicans in Paraguay.

There are also members of the Mormon, Jehovah's Witness, Church of God, Lutheran, and Methodist faiths in Paraguay. Most of these groups tend to focus on trying to convert others to their faith.

Immigration has also brought Muslims to Paraguay. The largest number of Muslims can be found in Ciudad del Este. The city supports two mosques, or Muslim places of worship. The best-known mosque is the Prophet Muhammad Mosque.

Paraguay is home to about a thousand Jews, most of whom live in Asunción.

The Fabric
of Culture

S OCIAL LIFE IN PARAGUAY IS CENTERED ON THE FAMILY.
The family provides an emotional safety net. Family can also be
counted on to help out in a time of need. Even distant relatives
are expected to be loyal and supportive. There is a tendency to
be suspicious of anyone not related by blood or marriage.

Opposite: **A farming family**

All in the Family

In Paraguay, children seldom leave home until they marry.
Single adults, especially women, who live alone are rare. A
newly married couple will sometimes live with one of the

**Family is at the heart of
Paraguayan culture.**

spouse's parents until
they can set up a house
on their own. In small
towns and rural areas, it is
common for couples to
live next door to their in-
laws. That way, children
can play with their
cousins, and many differ-
ent family members can
watch the children.

In the home, the man
is the head of the house-
hold. Fathers are treated
with respect, but they do

little around the house. They have little contact with the younger children. Men often go out in the evenings to socialize with their friends. Women, on the other hand, run the house. They cook, clean, do laundry, and take care of the kids. Mothers are the emotional anchors for their children, and their children adore them. When adult children return home, it is mostly to visit their mothers.

Young girls rarely date before they are fifteen. On their fifteenth birthday, a celebration called the *Quince Años* (fifteen years) is held in their honor. This includes a mass at the church. The girl wears a long white dress at the mass. A party is held afterward.

Paraguayan children remain close to their mothers even after they grow up.

Fiesta del Debut

When girls turn 16, a party called the Fiesta del Debut is given. This celebration is held to recognize that the girl is entering society as a woman. In the larger cities and among the middle and upper class, the event can be elegant. Several families may join together to present their daughters. The girls enter the room in beautiful gowns as their names and short biographies are read. Then everyone sits down to a delicious meal. After the meal, the tables are cleared and the room is converted to a disco. Sometimes the dancing continues until dawn.

In the rural areas and among the poor, expensive celebrations are not possible. Instead, girls are made to feel special with a small party in their home. It may include a good meal, a few small presents, guitar music, and singing.

After their Quince Años, girls may begin dating. In rural areas, dating is closely supervised. Girls are not allowed to go to parties or dances without a chaperone. The chaperone is usually the girl's mother or an older sister. The young man is expected to talk to the father and learn about the family. He is not allowed to spend time alone with the young woman in her home. Most people marry at an early age. People look down upon girls who are not married by a certain age.

The Paraguayan harp usually has thirty-six strings.

Harps, Guitars, and Native Sounds

Music has always been important to the people of Paraguay. The Guaraní Indians used wooden flutes, whistles, rattles, bells, and drums to reproduce the sounds and rhythms of the forest.

When the Spanish arrived with their guitars and harps, the Indians quickly adopted and modified the instruments. Working with the Jesuits, they converted the large European harps to smaller, lightweight instruments. The Indian harp, made of mahogany and pine, is now considered the national musical instrument of Paraguay. Almost all bands and orchestras include a Paraguayan harp. Radio stations in Paraguay must play at least one hour of harp music each day to keep their licenses.

Until the twentieth century, classical music in Paraguay meant European music. But then in the early 1900s, a young Paraguayan composer–guitarist named Agustín Barrios Mangoré began to make a significant impact. He composed music based on the traditions of native culture as well as classical European composers like Bach. He wanted to emphasize his Guaraní heritage, so he created a new image for his performances. He called himself Chief Nitsuga Mangoré. He gave concerts in full Guaraní tribal dress and considered himself a messenger of the Guaraní people. Classical guitarists throughout Latin America are indebted to this musical genius.

German composer Johann Sebastian Bach greatly influenced Paraguayan guitarist Agustín Barrios Mangoré.

José Asunción Flores (1904–1972) is credited with creating a new form of music in Paraguay. He made a romantic folk music called Guarania. Guarania incorporates tribal folk music and rhythms, and emphasizes the harp and guitars. It is a soft, romantic music that is often sad. Guarania music is for listening, not dancing.

Native folklore and religion are an important part of Paraguayan art. The Spanish missionaries taught the Indians to paint and carve. The Jesuits had art schools in the reducciones, and the Indians became master artists. They carved

Guitar music has long been popular in Paraguay.

Augusto Roa Bastos

The literature of Paraguay is dominated by writings that deal with the nation's social issues. The country's most noted literary figure is Augusto Roa Bastos. Bastos, who was born in 1917, took part in the Chaco War. This had a deep impact on his writing. He was a strong supporter of the poor and highly critical of Paraguayan dictators. One of his most famous novels is *I the Supreme*. It tells the story of the man who was elected dictator of Paraguay in 1814.

Bastos's political opinions forced him to leave the country in 1947. He lived in Argentina for many years and in France for a decade. In 1989, he was awarded the prestigious Cervantes Prize for Literature.

pulpits and seats in stone to be placed in the churches. They incorporated flowers, vines, trees, fruits, and animals into their work. These objects were mixed with images of the Virgin Mary, Jesus, and the saints.

The artistic skill of the Indians' work in stone is still visible at the Trinidad ruins. The best examples of their work are the magnificent high altars. These altars were carefully carved from the best hardwoods in the forest. One altar took decades to complete. Paraguay's churches remain museums for this unique and beautiful artwork.

The Church of Yaguarón

Yaguarón, which means "big jaguar" in Guaraní, is a peaceful village located about 30 miles (50 km) from Asunción. A mission was founded there in 1539. In 1640, the missionaries started building a church using Indian labor. The church was not completed until 1775. It took more than a century to build because all of the interior woodwork was carefully carved using tropical hardwoods. Even the wide outside corridors were designed with intricate wood carvings. The Indians made paint from local plants to decorate the interior. Many people believe this church is the most beautiful one in Paraguay. The site attracts thousands of tourists each year.

Handicrafts

Paraguay's most famous folk art is represented by *ñanduti*, or spider-web lace. The legend of its origin is very sad. A young bride found her groom dead in a small valley. She sat by him all night long. As dawn arrived, she saw that a spider had woven a silk blanket over her lover's body. She rushed home and embroidered a blanket like a spider web to cover him.

Itagua is the center of the ñanduti lace industry. People use ñanduti designs to create table centerpieces, mantle coverings, bridal veils, and bedcoverings. These designs are a mixture of Guaraní traditions and European lace-making techniques. Normally, fine cotton thread is used. White is the most common color. Ñanduti is a popular souvenir for tourists visiting Paraguay.

The caraguata fiber weavings of the Nivaclé Indians in the Chaco are also popular handicrafts. The Indians take the fibers from the leaves of the caraguata plant and place them in the sun to dry. Women artisans then take two strands of fiber and roll them across their thighs to make thread. The thread is dipped in pots of natural dye extracted from other local plants. Different roots, saps, bark, and leaves produce colors such as red, maroon, black, and gray. The dyed threads are then woven into beautiful bags and hammocks.

Ñanduti lace is noted for its complicated patterns.

The Daily Routine

IN PARAGUAY, THERE IS A BIG DIFFERENCE BETWEEN LIFE IN the country and life in the city. More than 40 percent of Paraguayans live in rural areas. Their lives are simple and filled with hard work. In the cities, people have more of a chance to go to school, get a good job, and enjoy modern life.

Despite these differences, rural and urban Paraguayans share many interests. They both consume huge amounts of a drink called *yerba maté*. They both have a passion for soccer. And they both love a good barbecue.

Opposite: **A market near the cathedral in Asunción**

Many Paraguayans love baseball.

National Holidays in Paraguay

January 1	New Year's Day
February 3	San Blas Day
February or March	Carnival
March 1	National Heroes Day
March or April	Good Friday to Easter Sunday
May 15	Independence Day
June 12	Chaco Armistice Day
August 15	Founding of Asunción
September 29	Victory of Boqueron Day
December 8	Virgin of Caacupé Day
December 25	Christmas Day

Many rural families live in wooden shacks.

Rural Life

Families in rural areas normally live in small houses with two to three rooms. The houses are usually made of wood or adobe brick, and have dirt floors and thatched roofs. Most small rural homes have no electricity, running water, or indoor bathrooms.

Farmers have small plots of land. Most of what they grow is consumed by the family. They also raise a few livestock. There is almost always a flock of chickens for meat and eggs. Some have a dairy cow for milk and a few pigs.

Life is not easy for small farmers. Everyone in the family is expected to work. The parents and children are up at dawn. After a short breakfast, they either go to school for four hours or to the fields. The first, third, and fifth graders go to school in the afternoons. When children are not at school, they are helping on the farm. It is more common for boys to work in the fields. Girls take care of younger children, help with cooking and cleaning, and sew.

In the evenings, men like to play soccer, bingo, and cards. They frequently drink beer or *caña*, a drink made from sugarcane, while they play. Women do not have much free time. Their major recreation is talking with other women. Sometimes they get together to bake or to do their laundry at the river. Boys play soccer and volleyball, and girls jump rope or play *tikichuelas*. Tikichuelas is similar to jacks except the players use rocks as jacks and a small unripened fruit called a guavira as the ball.

All across Paraguay, people drink yerba maté.

A kitchen in Paraguay

Urban Life

Life is easier in Asunción and other larger cities than it is in the country. Most homes are still small, just two to four rooms, and they have concrete floors and tile roofs. Most homes also have electricity, running water, and indoor bathrooms. It is a different world on the hills surrounding Asunción. There, a small number of wealthy families live in lavish mansions.

Pelota-tata (Fireball)

One of Paraguay's most popular national festivals is the Festival of San Juan. Families celebrate all day long. Just before dark, the children begin to get excited. They know that the time for *pelota-tata* is very near. This is a dangerous but thrilling game. Adults make balls out of twigs and rags. Then they soak them in kerosene, a type of oil. As soon as it is dark, they light the balls on fire and throw them into the crowd. The air is filled with screams and laughter as children and teenagers kick the fiery ball around the crowd. The loudest shrieks are heard when the pelota-tata heads for the old women in lawn chairs. As soon as the fireball burns out, someone else launches another. The thrilling action goes on late into the night.

Not everyone in the city is so fortunate, however. Miserable slums line the river that passes through Asunción. The houses are made of plywood, cardboard, tin, and whatever other scraps the builder can find. These houses do not have electricity or running water.

In the cities, men normally work in factories that produce food products, beverages, leather, plastics, soap, and other things. Some men work in banking, insurance, and management. Their wives usually remain at home, where they take care of the house and children. In recent years, some women have taken jobs to improve the family income.

Thousands of families live in slums along the Río Paraguay.

Life for children in the cities is easier than that of their rural cousins. They go to school, do a few chores, and play with their friends. Many children, both boys and girls, play sports. Soccer, basketball, and volleyball are all popular. Children often take music lessons, learning to play the guitar or the piano.

Children from the slums have a much harder time. They frequently work after school at odd jobs to earn a little money. They shine shoes, wash windshields at traffic lights, sell snacks on street corners, or beg.

Social life in the city is much more exciting than in the country. Asunción is full of wonderful restaurants. Casinos offer the chance to gamble. Discos and dance clubs dot the city. Many Paraguayans love to stay up until the wee hours of the morning.

More than 40 percent of Paraguayans live in poor or overcrowded houses.

Yerba maté is also known as Paraguay tea.

The National Drink

Both rural and urban Paraguayans drink yerba maté. It is at the center of social life in Paraguay. Yerba maté is a tea-like drink produced from the leaves and stem of the yerba maté plant. This plant is an evergreen member of the holly family. The Guaraní Indians considered it sacred and used it long before the Spanish arrived. The Jesuits grew the yerba maté plant on the reducciones.

To make the drink, the plant's leaves and small stems are picked and dried. They are then crushed and placed in the bottom of a *maté*. The maté is a cup traditionally made from a gourd or a cow's horn. The leaves are steeped in hot water. Paraguayans sip the drink through a *bombilla*, a straw that is usually made of metal or wood. The bombilla has a filter on the end, which prevents the crushed leaves and stems from being sucked into the drinker's mouth. Frequently, a group of Paraguayans will sit and discuss politics or soccer while passing a single maté around the group. It would be considered very rude to refuse a drink when it is offered in this manner.

Yerba maté is a refreshing drink served hot in cool weather and cold in hot weather. It contains many important vitamins and minerals. The Indians believed that it cleaned their blood, gave them stamina, and made them mentally alert. Today, health food stores in the United States promote the drink as an alternative to coffee and tea.

Four Meals a Day

Paraguayans typically eat four meals a day: breakfast, lunch, *marienda*, and dinner. Marienda is similar to the English teatime. It is served in the afternoon at around four o'clock. At marienda, people eat bread, cookies, or other sweet foods along with coffee or tea.

Cassava roots are longer than potatoes.

One of the most common foods in Paraguay is cassava. Cassava is a root vegetable that is generally peeled like a potato and boiled. The cooked root is then diced and mashed until it produces a doughlike substance. This dough is used to make the crust on little pies called empanadas. The empanadas may be filled with ground beef, cheese, boiled eggs, spinach, or other meats and vegetables. The dough is folded over the ingredients and pressed shut. The

The National Dish

Sopa Paraguaya (Paraguayan soup) is the national dish. In reality, it is neither a soup nor a stew. It is more like a pudding. It is a mixture of onion, grated cheese, eggs, cornmeal, pork fat, baking powder, salt, pepper, and sometimes a tomato. The mixture is then placed in a pan and baked in an oven until brown. During Lent, the time before Easter, most Paraguayans give up meat dishes. Sopa Paraguaya is popular at that time of year. It is almost always served at weddings.

empanada is then dropped into hot cooking oil until it turns golden brown.

Corn is another mainstay of the Paraguayan diet. It is used to make cornbread, corn dumplings, and the popular *chipa guasu*, which is a creamy onion custard. Many times, the cook will mix grated cheese into the cornbread to add flavor.

Barbecued meat is a staple of the Paraguayan diet.

Cooking meat is considered an art in Paraguay. The most popular technique is to grill the meat at outdoor barbecues called *asadas*. Beef, pork, chicken, and lamb are all popular meats at asadas. Meats are also used in soups and stews. Along the major rivers, fish are often eaten, especially *dorado*, *surubi*, and *pacu*.

Paraguayans love the abundant fruit that grows in their country. Most people eat fruit at several meals every day. Among the favorites are mangoes, pineapples, grapefruit, oranges, and avocados. In rural areas, a popular drink is sugarcane juice.

Education

Children must go to school for six years in Paraguay. Most children start school when they are seven years old. The school year begins in March and ends in December. There is a two-week winter vacation in July. The regular school day lasts for four hours, from 7:00 A.M. until 11:00 A.M. If the school is crowded, they may run a second shift from 1:00 P.M. to 5:00 P.M.

Children study math, science, reading, and grammar. Classes must be taught in Spanish for at least three hours a day. There is usually one class in Guaraní. Some schools offer

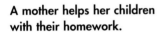
A mother helps her children with their homework.

Secondary school students celebrate Independence Day.

art classes, music, and physical education. Most schools cannot afford books or other teaching materials. Teachers write information on blackboards, and students copy the information into their notebooks. They are graded on how well they memorize the information.

Secondary schools include grades seven through twelve. Only about one-quarter of Paraguayan children attend secondary schools, and few finish. Most secondary schools are in urban areas. Few rural children go beyond the sixth grade.

Paraguay has two major universities in Asunción. The National University, which is run by the government, is free. More than 25,000 students attend the school. The National University also has branches in other cities such as Ciudad del Este and Encarnación. Catholic University of Our Lady of Asunción is a private university with approximately 10,000 students.

Paraguayans are passionate about soccer.

Sports

Soccer (*fútbol*) is king in Paraguay. The players on the national team are heroes to an adoring public. No other sport comes close to challenging soccer for the public's attention. The British brought soccer to Paraguay in the late 1800s. Olimpia, the first club, was founded in 1902. Team Guaraní followed a year later. In 1906, the Paraguayan Football League Association was established. Several more clubs were quickly created.

Paraguay started participating in the *Copa America* (American Cup) in 1921. The next year, the team finished as a runner-up to powerful Brazil. Over the next thirty-three years, Paraguay's team finished second four times. They won the championship in 1953 and again in 1979. These accomplishments are remarkable considering that Paraguay was playing such world powers as Brazil, Argentina, Mexico, and Chile. Brazil's population is 183 million, while Paraguay's is only 6 million. Still, the Brazilian team always knew they were

José Luis Chilavert

"Chilaaaaaa, Chilaaaaaaa . . ."—this name echoes across the playing field and through the streets of the most remote villages. José Luis Chilavert is almost a god in Paraguay. He was the goalkeeper on Paraguay's national soccer team until he retired in 2004. During his career, Chilavert scored sixty goals on free kicks and penalty shots, an incredible feat for a goalkeeper. Chilavert was charismatic, aggressive, and had a legendary temper. He also had the distinct ability to intimidate opposing players. Twice he was named South American Player of the Year. Some people believe he is the best player in the history of Paraguayan soccer.

in for a fight when they played the Guaraníes, the nickname for the national team.

Looking Toward the Future

In Paraguay, people are looking toward a brighter future. Parents hope that their children can get an education and improve the quality of their lives. The nation has great hope that the democracy established by the 1992 constitution will continue to blossom. They look forward to an improved economy that will increase their standard of living. Paraguayans are proud of their national identity. And they are eager for the rest of the world to learn more about them.

Timeline

Paraguayan History

Paraguay declares independence from Spain.	1811
José Gaspar Rodríguez de Francia becomes dictator of Paraguay and isolates the nation.	1814
Carlos Antonio López rules Paraguay; he eliminates some of Francia's strict laws and reopens the country.	1840–1862
Francisco Solano López becomes Paraguay's dictator.	1862
The War of the Triple Alliance begins.	1865
Francisco López is killed, ending the War of the Triple Alliance.	1870
Paraguay fights the Chaco War with Bolivia.	1932–1935
General Alfredo Stroessner seizes power in a military coup.	1954
Stroessner is thrown out of office in a military coup. General Andres Rodríguez replaces Stroessner.	1989
A new, democratic constitution is ratified.	1992
Democratic elections are held.	1993
Vice president Luis María Argaña is assassinated.	1999
Nicanor Duarte Frutos is elected president.	2003

World History

1865	The American Civil War ends.
1914	World War I breaks out.
1917	The Bolshevik Revolution brings communism to Russia.
1929	Worldwide economic depression begins.
1939	World War II begins, following the German invasion of Poland.
1945	World War II ends.
1957	The Vietnam War starts.
1969	Humans land on the moon.
1975	The Vietnam War ends.
1979	Soviet Union invades Afghanistan.
1983	Drought and famine in Africa.
1989	The Berlin Wall is torn down, as communism crumbles in Eastern Europe.
1991	Soviet Union breaks into separate states.
1992	Bill Clinton is elected U.S. president.
2000	George W. Bush is elected U.S. president.
2001	Terrorists attack World Trade Towers, New York and the Pentagon, Washington, D.C.

Fast Facts

Official name: Republic of Paraguay

Capital: Asunción

Official languages: Spanish and Guaraní

Asunción

Paraguay's flag

Bottle tree

Year of founding:	1811
National anthem:	*Himno Nacional*
Type of government:	Constitutional republic
Head of state:	President
Geographic center:	23°S, 58°W
Bordering countries:	Argentina, Brazil, and Bolivia
Highest elevation:	Near Villarrica, 2,762 feet (842 m) above sea level
Lowest elevation:	The junction of the Río Paraguay and the Río Paraná, 150 feet (46 m) above sea level
Average temperature:	73°F (22.8°C)
Average precipitation:	70 inches (178 cm) in eastern Paraguay, 20 inches (51 cm) in western Paraguay
National population (2004 est.):	6,000,000

Population of largest cities (2003):

Asunción	539,200
Ciudad del Este	223,400
Luque	170,400
Capiatá	154,500
Lambare	120,000

Ruins of La Santísima
Trinidad de Paraná

Paraguayan currency

Famous landmarks:
- ▶ *Itaipú Dam*, Hernandarias
- ▶ *Metropolitan Cathedral*, Asunción
- ▶ *La Santísima Trinidad de Paraná*, Encarnación
- ▶ *Mennonite colonies*, Filadelfia
- ▶ *Pantheon of Heroes*, Asunción

Industry: Paraguay is Latin America's largest exporter of electricity. The industrial sector of Paraguay's economy is poorly developed. Food processing and beverage production are the most common manufacturing activities. Mining contributes very little to the economy.

Currency: The Guaraní is the national currency of Paraguay. One U.S. dollar is equal to 6,250 Guaraní.

Weights and measures: The metric system

Literacy rate: 93 percent (1999 estimate)

A Paraguayan family

Augusto Roa Bastos

Common words and phrases:

Spanish	Guaraní	English
Adiós	*Tereiko pora*	Good-bye
Buenos días	*Mba'e'ichapa ne ko'e*	Good morning
Cuánto?	*Mbovy'pa?*	How much?
Dónde?	*Mamo'pa?*	Where?
Habla español?	*Mezcla de espanol?*	Do you speak Spanish?
Gracias	*Aguyje*	Thank you
No es posible	*Ndikatu'i*	It is not possible
Es muy sabroso?	*Heve tisyrygui?*	Does it taste good?
Grande	*Guasu*	Big

Famous Paraguayans:

Augusto Roa Bastos *Writer, political activist*	(1917–)
José Luis Chilavert *Soccer player*	(1965–)
José Asunción Flores *Musician and creator of* *Guarania music*	(1904–1972)
José Gaspar Rodríguez de Francia *Dictator*	(1790–1840)
Domingo Martínez de Irala *Spanish governor of Paraguay*	(1486–1557)
General Alfredo Stroessner *Dictator*	(1912–)

To Find Out More

Nonfiction

▶ Hernández, Roger E. *Paraguay*. Philadelphia: Mason Crest, 2004.

▶ Jermyn, Leslie. *Paraguay*. New York: Marshall Cavendish, 2000.

▶ Morrison, Marion. *Paraguay*. Philadelphia: Chelsea House, 2000.

Music

▶ *Explorer: Paraguay—Guaraní Songs and Dances*. Nonesuch, 2003.

▶ Williams, John. *From the Jungles of Paraguay*. Sony, 1995. (John Williams plays the music of Agustín Barrios Mangoré, Paraguay's most famous composer–musician.)

Web Sites

▶ **Peace Corps Destination: Paraguay**
http://www.peacecorps.gov/wws/
guides/paraguay/overview.html
*General information, maps, videos,
lesson plans, and interviews with Peace
Corps workers.*

▶ **Museo del Barro**
http://www.museodelbarro.org.py/
html/MenuIngles.html
*This site provides a tour of the Museo
del Barro in Asunción, which focuses
on the art of Paraguay.*

Organizations and Embassies

▶ **Embassy of the Republic
of Paraguay**
2400 Massachusetts Avenue, NW
Washington, DC 20008
(202) 483-6960

Index

Page numbers in *italics* indicate illustrations.

Meet the Author

BYRON AUGUSTIN is a professor of geography at Texas State University in San Marcos, Texas. His love for geography has instilled in him a passion for traveling abroad. He has visited forty-nine of the fifty United States, twenty-six of Mexico's thirty-one states, and eight Canadian provinces. Augustin has also toured fifty-four countries on five of the seven continents.

Augustin is a professional photographer as well. More than 1,200 of his photos have been published worldwide. The National Geographic Society, *Encyclopædia Britannica*, *Outdoor Life*, and scores of books and magazines have published his photographs. More than a dozen books in the Enchantment of the World Series feature his photos. He is the author of *Bolivia*, *Panama*, and the *United Arab Emirates*, and he and his wife, Rebecca, co-authored *Qatar*.

Writing the book about Paraguay was a special treat. Augustin teaches a course on the geography of Latin America and has been reading about and researching Paraguay for more than thirty years. To write this book, he used the superb library facilities on his own university campus as well as the public library in New Braunfels, Texas. He also searched on the Internet and reviewed 110 years of *National Geographic* magazine. Much of the statistical data was provided by Paraguayan government agencies. Interviews with Paraguayan students attending Texas State University were another important source of information.

Photo Credits